How To Be a Science Superhero

This edition first published in MMXVIII by
Book House

Distributed by Black Rabbit Books
P.O. Box 3263
Mankato, Minnesota 56002

Cataloging-in-Publication Data is available
from the Library of Congress

Printed in the United States
At Corporate Graphics,
North Mankato, Minnesota

9 8 7 6 5 4 3 2 1

ISBN: 978-1-911242-72-7

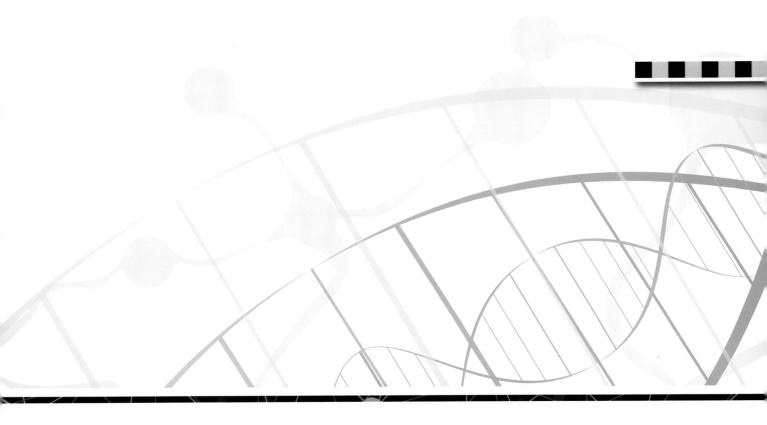

ZAP!

How To Be a Science
Superhero

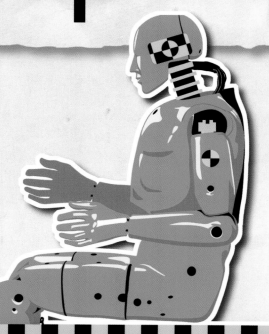

Richard & Louise
Spilsbury

Contents

The Science of Superpowers

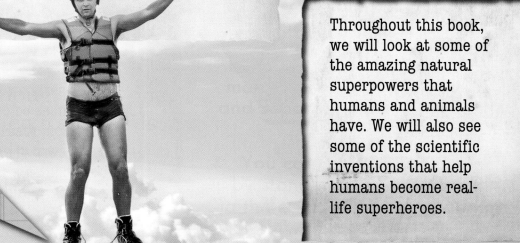

Superheroes are imaginary characters that have superhuman powers. Superheroes are often exceptionally strong. They can be invisible, and they can create **force fields**, survive disasters, and see through things. Science can show us how these superpowers can exist in the real world.

Jetpacks

The invention of the jetpack allows individual humans to fly without an aircraft. The water jetpack shoots water downward so the wearer is propelled upward.

Throughout this book, we will look at some of the amazing natural superpowers that humans and animals have. We will also see some of the scientific inventions that help humans become real-life superheroes.

The flyboard water jetpack is connected to a Jet Ski® by a bendy tube about 59 feet (18 meters) long.

The Jet Ski's engine thrusts water at high speed down the tube.

The water shooting out of two nozzles in the bottom pushes up the flyboard.

Flyboarders can shoot 49 feet (15 meters) into the air. That is as high as a six-story building.

The Power of Invisibility

In the Middle Ages, some people tried to become invisible by covering their bodies in a mixture of crushed owl's eye, beetle dung, and olive oil. Luckily, today there are less smelly options.

People cannot disappear or become invisible like a superhero, but they can trick others into thinking they have. **Camouflage** that soldiers wear is a good example of this.

How Camouflage Works

Camouflage suits work by deceiving the human eye. They use contrasts of light and dark colors that match the background terrain—for example, green for forests and brown for deserts. The colors are in mottled patterns that break up the sharp lines between colors, which are easy for eyes to detect.

Stealth planes have heat shields to avoid heat-sensing missiles.

Stealth Planes

Stealth planes have flat surfaces and sharp edges that deflect **radar** waves to help them stay invisible in the sky. Any radar waves that do reflect from the plane are focused into a few bright rays, which are difficult for detectors to lock on to.

Bending Light

Scientists are working on a special type of fabric that could make soldiers vanish. The fabric would work by bending light waves around the wearer so that he or she cannot be seen. This would change the face of warfare because it could allow soldiers to carry out raids in broad daylight without detection.

Stealth planes are coated with substances that absorb radar waves.

Parts in a cuttlefish's skin called chromatophores allow the fish to change their appearance.

Animal Inspiration

Scientists are studying animals, such as the cuttlefish, to improve camouflage suits. The cuttlefish can alter both the color and pattern of its skin, helping it to instantly blend in with new surroundings to avoid **predators**.

Cuttlefish can change color in less than a second.

Crashproof

The very best way to survive a car crash is not to have an accident in the first place. Safe, careful, and confident driving can help people avoid crashes.

If the worst happens, drivers can minimize their chances of sustaining a serious injury by wearing a seat belt. They can also stow away loose items that might hit them if they suddenly stopped. It is also better to travel in cars fitted with **airbags**.

Seat Belts

English engineer Sir George Cayley invented the seat belt in the mid-nineteenth century. However, the retractable seat belt used today was not fully developed until 1959. The Swedish inventor Nils Bohlin tested it for the car company Volvo. He discovered that it increased the chances of survival in an accident.

Safety First

1. Do not drive too close to the car in front.
2. Move away from a car that is on fire.
3. Drive carefully on winding country roads.
4. Cars on tow trucks may not be properly secured, so keep a safe distance.
5. Be careful around much larger vehicles.
6. Watch out for broken-down cars.
7. Drive carefully on narrow roads.
8. Look out for pedestrians.
9. Airbags may save your life in a head-on collision.

Road traffic injuries are the main cause of death among young people ages 15–29 years.

Crash Test Dummies

Crash test dummies are used to test the safety of new vehicles. They simulate the impact of a car accident on the human body. The first crash test dummies were dead bodies. The modern dummy, Hybrid III, was first introduced in 1976.

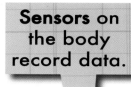

Sensors on the body record data.

Marks measure the movement of the head.

The **joints** are highly lifelike.

The Side Impact Dummy (SID) is designed to test injuries sustained during side-on collisions.

A Family of Dummies

There is now a whole family of crash test dummies of varying sizes commonly used in tests. These include two adult males, a fairly short adult female, and three children of ten, six, and three years old.

About 1.25 million people die each year as a result of road traffic accidents.

Sub-Zero
Superpowers

When it is hot, humans perspire (sweat) to cool down. Water released through skin pores **evaporates** from the body, and as it does so, it takes some of the warmth away, too. If people use a fan, the air blowing over the skin speeds up the process of evaporation, helping them to feel even cooler.

On humid days, perspiration evaporates more slowly because the air already contains a lot of water. That is why it is harder for people to stay cool when humidity is high.

Sweat Facts

- The human body has between two and four million sweat **glands**.

- People have the most sweat glands on the bottoms of their feet.

- Humans produce about 0.3 gallon (1 liter) of sweat every day, but because it evaporates quickly, they do not notice it.

Primates and horses have armpits that sweat like human armpits.

Animal Tactics

Animals have different ways to stay cool. They wallow in water or mud to stay cool. Dogs get rid of excess heat by **panting**. Some animals burrow underground out of the sun or become **dormant** to avoid a hot season.

Insulation

People may not realize it, but **insulation** keeps things cool as well as warm. The insulation used in attics is made of fluffy materials that reflect and block heat and light from entering. The materials also stop cooler air that comes in through windows left open at night from escaping during the day.

Dogs expel hot breath as fast as they can and inhale cooler air.

Cool Transport

Human organs are usually transported between hospitals for transplant operations in an ice-cold **preservative** solution in insulated boxes. On long trips, the organs may be moved between a fridge, a refrigerated truck, and cool boxes in order to reach the patient in time.

A new organ cool box design keeps a donor heart pumping until it is placed in a patient.

Feel the Force

A force field is an invisible barrier of **force**—a force that affects something without touching it. Gravity is an invisible force. Earth is so big that its gravity pulls everything on or near its surface toward its center.

Gravity is the force that pulls someone back to the ground every time he or she jumps. Gravity is also the force that gives everything on Earth weight.

Static Electricity

Static electricity makes an electrical force field. **Atoms** inside materials contain **electrons** that have an electric **charge**. When materials rub together, electrons move from one to another, creating static electricity that can pull on things. Static electricity can be seen when people comb their hair. When they do this, they rub some electrons off their hair and onto the comb. When the comb has more electrons than the hair, static electricity pulls the hair toward the comb.

Some animals contain magnetic material and navigate using Earth's **magnetic field**.

Magnetism

Magnets work on metals, such as iron. A magnet's force is strongest near its ends, called north and south **poles**. Different poles attract each other. A south pole of one magnet and a north pole of another magnet pull together. Like poles (poles that are the same) repel each other. If you put two north or two south poles near each other, they push apart.

Electromagnetism

An **electromagnet** is a magnet that is created using electricity. Electricity can be turned on and off, and so can an electromagnet. Electromagnets are used in many electric devices, such as speakers, motors, and generators. They are also used on cranes to lift and drop iron and steel in junkyards.

Maglev trains can travel at 311 miles per hour (500 kilometers per hour).

No wheels means less friction and faster speeds for Maglev trains.

Floating Trains

Maglev is short for magnetic levitation. Maglev trains use an electromagnetic charge to move without touching the guideway rails on the ground.

Maglev trains can travel twice as fast as conventional commuter trains.

X-Ray Vision

Some superheroes can see through walls. There are machines that allow people to see inside the body.

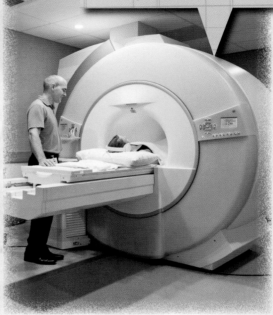

A CT scanner takes multiple X-ray images of the inside of a patient's body.

X-rays are light waves that people cannot see or feel.

X-Rays

German scientist Wilhelm Rontgen discovered X-rays in 1895. X-rays are light waves that can travel through skin, fat, and **muscle**. They cannot go through hard parts of the body, such as bones and teeth. That is how doctors can use X-rays to make photographs of broken bones and decaying teeth.

CT Scans

Computerised Tomography (CT) scanners take hundreds of X-ray pictures of a patient's body, slice by slice. A computer uses these **2D** images to produce a **3D** image that allows doctors to view the inside of the patient's body from different angles, helping to diagnose conditions such as bone damage, injuries to internal organs, problems with blood flow, strokes, and diseases, such as cancer.

At first, many X-ray machines were used to find bullets in human bodies.

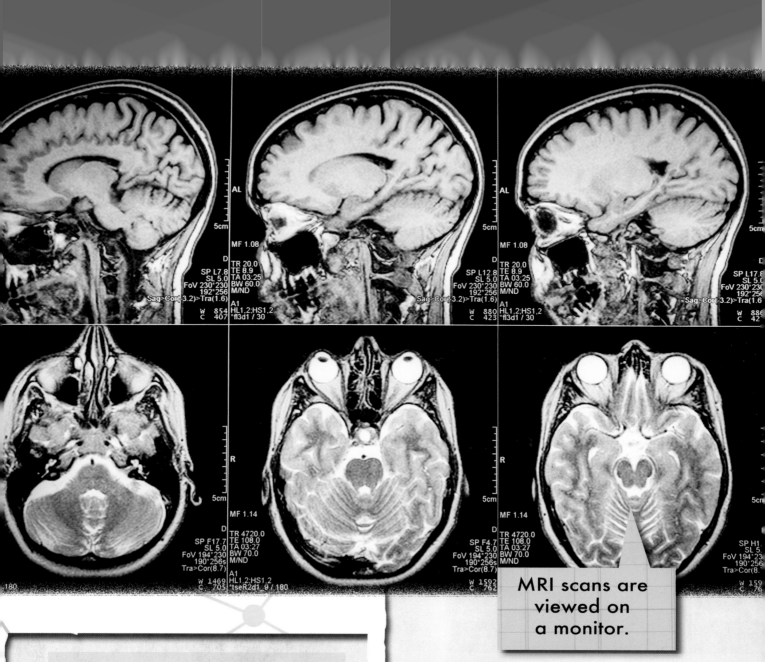

MRI scans are viewed on a monitor.

Ultrasound Scans

Ultrasound scanners have been used since the 1960s to check on babies inside their mothers' wombs. High-frequency sound waves are sent through the pregnant woman's stomach. These waves reflect off the soft organs of the baby inside, and bounce back as echoes. These are displayed as moving images on a monitor.

MRI Scans

Magnetic Resonance Imaging (MRI) scanners were first used in the 1970s. When inside an MRI scanner, a patient is surrounded by a **magnetic field** and scanned with radio waves. Atoms inside the body absorb the radio waves and send out radio signals that the scanner can use to create 3D images of a patient's internal organs and the **cells** that cause disease.

An MRI magnet creates a field up to 4,000 times stronger than Earth's magnetic field.

Regeneration

Scientists cannot create whole new bodies yet, but with people living longer than ever, it is becoming important to find ways to replace parts of the human body as they wear out.

The human body can already renew parts of itself. New skin cells form to renew the surface layer of the skin every two to four weeks.

Stem Cells

Stem cells can develop into any kind of cell in the human body. Scientists use stem cells to grow body parts. To grow a nose, doctors can take stem cells from a patient's fat and grow it over a nose mold. Then, they implant the nose into the patient's body so that skin grows over it. Once it is ready, they attach the nose to the face.

Cells

The human body makes new cells by mitosis. Mitosis is when one cell makes an exact copy of itself and divides into two identical cells. One skin cell can divide to make two; those two then divide to make four; those four split to make eight, and so on.

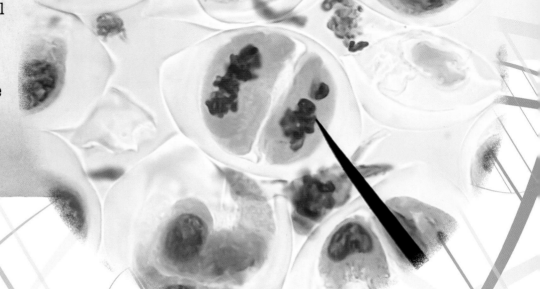

The cells in the human stomach last only two days before they need to be replaced.

In order to regrow a leg, salamanders use cells that can develop into different types of cell.

Help From Salamanders

Salamanders can regrow body parts, such as a tail or leg, when they break off. Scientists are studying how salamander cells do this to see if they can use that knowledge to help humans regenerate whole limbs by themselves one day.

Clones

In 1996, Dolly the sheep became the first ever mammal to be cloned. Scientists extracted DNA from one of her cells and inserted that DNA into a new cell. The sheep that developed from the new cell was exactly the same as Dolly because all its genetic information came from one parent cell, rather than a mix of two parent cells as usually happens with mammals. Could scientists clone humans one day, too?

Salamanders can lose a tail or leg to escape predators.

The Power of Superstrength

Superheroes often have large muscles, but muscles do not need to be supersized to be strong. To make strong muscles, people need to eat a variety of nutritious foods and exercise regularly.

Muscles are made up of muscle fibers. Exercise makes muscles stronger and bigger because it makes the muscle fibers thicker. Strong muscles work more efficiently and they have more **stamina**.

Muscles, Bones, and Joints

Muscles are attached to bones, which they pull on to move the body. Bones are connected to other bones at flexible joints, such as the elbows or knees. In ball-and-socket joints, such as the shoulder, a bone with a ball-shaped end fits inside a bone with a cup-shaped end. These joints allow movement in every direction.

To bend your arm, the biceps muscle contracts.

It takes around 17 muscles to smile and an average of 43 muscles to frown.

How Muscles Work

Muscles can only pull. When a muscle pulls, it **contracts**. The muscle becomes shorter and harder. When a muscle relaxes, it stops pulling and gets longer and softer again. To make bones move, each of the muscles in a pair pulls in a different direction.

When the biceps muscle contracts, it stretches the triceps.

The triceps contracts to straighten the arm again.

Weight-Bearing Exercise

Weight-bearing exercises that require people to lift their own body weight or work against a resistance are especially good for muscles. These include gymnastics, rock climbing, skipping, and sports, such as soccer, tennis, and basketball.

Warm-Ups

It is vital to warm up before exercising by doing 5 minutes of gentle activity, like walking, jogging, or stretching. This loosens the muscles and gets the blood flowing. Warming up prevents muscle strain and torn muscles.

There are more than 600 muscles in the body, and most actions use many muscles simultaneously.

Super Immunity

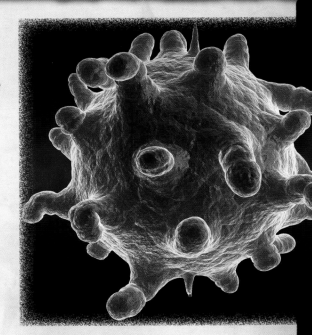

Colds are spread by **viruses**. A virus is a microorganism— a living thing too small for the human eye to see.

Once the virus gets inside the body's cells, it uses the host's own cells to make millions of new viruses. Your body uses coughs, sneezes, and a runny nose to try to get the germs out of its system.

How Colds Spread

The virus microorganisms that cause colds are spread in air when people cough or sneeze. If someone coughs on his or her hand and touches a handle, the next person to touch that handle, and then put his or her fingers close to their nose, eyes, or mouth, will become infected, too.

A sneeze can send droplets carrying the cold virus up to 11.5 feet (3.5 meters) away.

There are more than 200 different viruses that can give you a cold.

Fighting Viruses

The best way to stop colds is for people to sneeze or cough into a tissue and throw away the tissue. After this, they should wash their hands. Hands spread around eight out of ten common infections, so if everyone washed their hands more often and more carefully, there would be fewer colds.

Antibiotics

Antibiotics are special medicines designed to kill **bacteria**. They have no effect on viral infections because they cannot destroy viruses. Most viruses cannot be treated with medicines. Patients have to wait until their **immune systems** cure them.

The Immune System

When people get a viral disease, like chicken pox, their white blood cells make **antibodies** that destroy the virus. The antibodies stay in the blood, ready to destroy similar viruses in the future. However, there are many different cold viruses, so, although our bodies create antibodies to fight the virus that caused one cold, the next cold may be caused by a different type.

Virus droplets can survive for up to 48 hours on a surface.

A sneeze can send 100,000 virus-containing droplets into the air.

Superintelligence

Being intelligent is not just about knowing facts. Some people have **interpersonal** intelligence and are good with people. Others are good at expressing themselves, at solving problems, at judging distances and space, or have great musical or language abilities.

People can all learn to do things more intelligently by resisting the urge to ask other people to do things for them and figuring it out by themselves instead.

Improve Your Memory

When people say someone is intelligent, what they often mean is that they can remember a lot of facts. People can make themselves seem smarter by improving their ability to remember things. Brain games are puzzles that help people learn how to memorize faces, objects, and numbers more easily. People can also practice techniques that help them remember lists and facts more quickly.

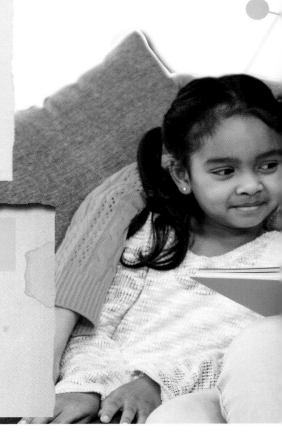

Read More

By reading more, whether it is books, magazines, online articles, or newspapers, people will discover more ideas and information. It is not about reading quickly but rather about reading thoughtfully and taking in what is read. That way, people will learn and remember more.

Doctors believe that exercise and keeping fit improves memory.

Try It Yourself

Here are some things you can do to boost your brain:
- Learn a new word each day.
- Take up a new hobby.
- Join a new class.
- Learn a new language.
- Play a musical instrument.

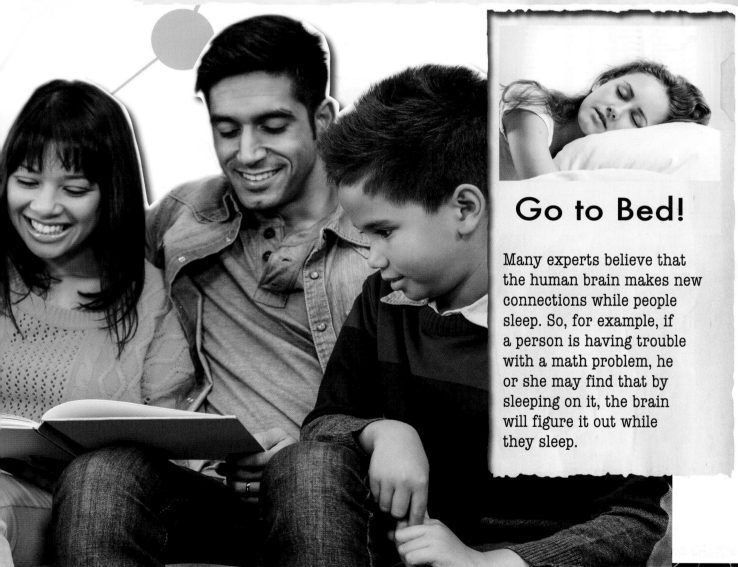

Go to Bed!

Many experts believe that the human brain makes new connections while people sleep. So, for example, if a person is having trouble with a math problem, he or she may find that by sleeping on it, the brain will figure it out while they sleep.

A good night's sleep can improve test scores without a student doing any extra work.

Longevity

No one can live forever. The **genes** of each species (type) of animal, including humans, program them to live for a certain number of years, as long as they do not get a disease or have a fatal accident. The average lifespan of a human is around 70 years.

As a result of improved diet and healthcare, more and more people are living longer. A person's best chances of living to 100 years or older are to live a healthy lifestyle and to take good care of him or herself.

Take Care of Yourself

- Do not take unnecessary risks.
- Wear safety equipment, such as seat belts and helmets.
- Drink plenty of water.
- Avoid stress and make time to relax.
- Get at least eight hours of sleep a night.
- Have regular checkups with a doctor.
- Do not smoke.

When you sleep, your body puts energy into fighting off infections and healing.

Move to Japan

People in Japan usually live longer than people in other countries. Factors that increase their **life expectancy** include a diet high in fish, vegetables, and pulses (beans, peas, and lentils), and low in salt.

Animal Lifespans

Bowhead whale	200 years
Galápagos tortoise	177 years
African elephant	70 years
Grizzly bear	40 years
Horse	62 years
Mouse	3 years
Bat	2 years

Most Japanese people also walk and bike when they can.

Japanese people are very careful about hygiene and cleanliness.

Relaxation techniques such as **yoga** and **Tai Chi** are popular in Japan.

Switch Off the Aging Genes

One thing that determines how long people live is the genes that they inherit from their parents. Scientists are trying to discover which genes in the human body are most responsible for aging. In theory, if they can turn off these aging genes, it might mean they could lengthen the human lifespan.

The record for the oldest person ever is Jeanne Louise Calment. She died at 122 years, 164 days.

The Power of Telepathy

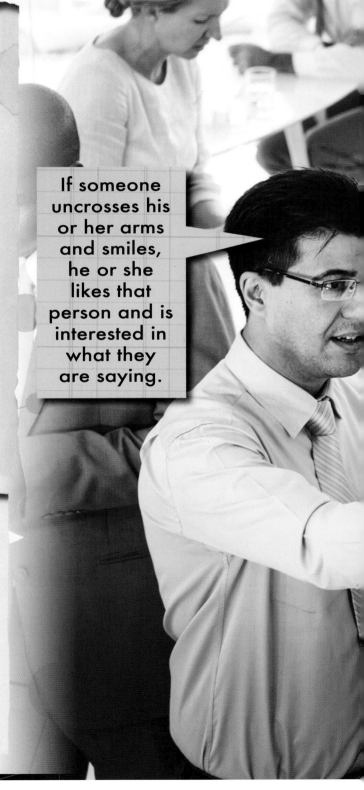

For many people, being a mind reader would be their top superpower choice. However, people do not need to be mind readers to know another person's thoughts without being told what they are.

The first step is for people to listen more carefully and to concentrate on the speaker without interruption. They should think about what the person is saying and listen to his or her tone of voice, rather than thinking about what they are going to say.

If someone uncrosses his or her arms and smiles, he or she likes that person and is interested in what they are saying.

Body Language

Body language is when people express their thoughts, intentions, or feelings by the way they stand, the way they hold their arms, and the faces they make when they speak to other people. Body language can often reveal more than words alone.

Facial Expressions

Facial expressions can reveal truths. For example, if the eyes do not smile when the mouth does, it is a fake smile. When people frown, look away, or narrow their eyes, they are feeling unfriendly. Look out for micro-expressions, too. These are involuntary facial expressions that may last a fraction of a second but give away people's real feelings before they react the way they want you to see!

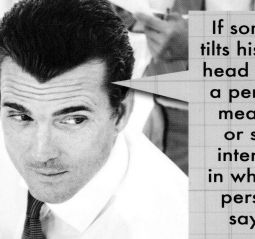

If someone tilts his or her head toward a person, it means he or she is interested in what that person is saying.

Locked-In Syndrome

People with locked-in syndrome cannot speak and are totally **paralyzed**. Scientists have invented a real-life mind-reading machine that allows these patients to communicate. **Electrodes** attached to patients' heads analyze electrical signals in their brains to work out what they are thinking.

Detectives use body language to read suspects' minds.

Disasterproof

Lightning is a giant spark of electricity between clouds or between a cloud and the ground. As pieces of ice swirling inside storm clouds knock against each other, they build up an electrical charge. This can make a spark that suddenly jumps toward Earth as a flash of lightning.

A bolt of lightning can carry temperatures around five times hotter than the Sun. Lightning can set buildings on fire and cause severe burns or even death. Lightning can also cause trees to explode.

There are lightning flashes in Earth's atmosphere about 50 times per second or 4.3 million times a day.

Thunder and Lightning

The loud bang (thunder) happens because a flash of lightning heats up the air around it, causing it to expand. The thunderclap is heard after the lightning because sound travels more slowly through air than light does.

Every year, around 50 people in the United States alone die as a result of being struck by lightning.

Keep Safe

If people are caught outside in a thunderstorm, they should take shelter in a building, under a bus shelter, or in a car. They should never take shelter under trees because trees attract lightning. Many buildings are protected by metal rods called lightning **conductors**. Lightning conductors bring lightning from the top of a building safely into the ground.

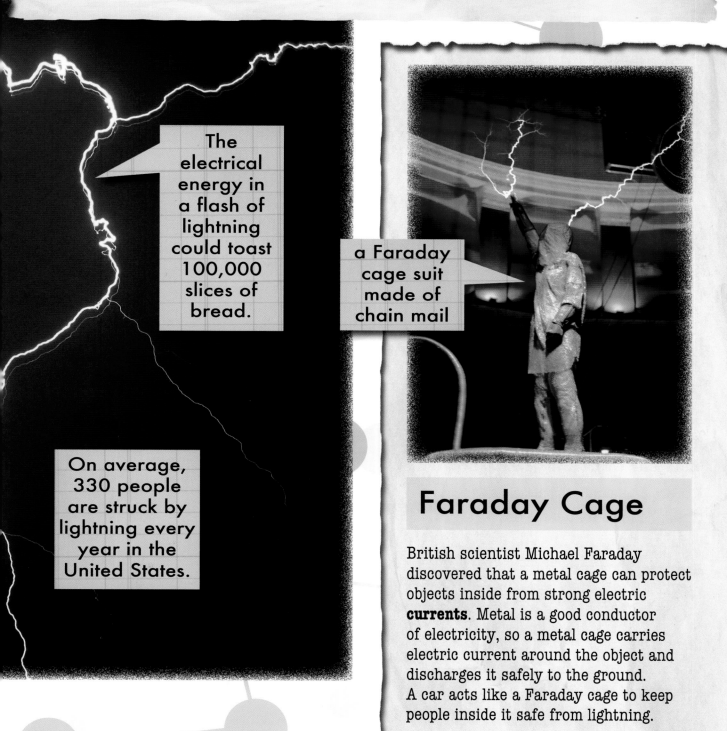

The electrical energy in a flash of lightning could toast 100,000 slices of bread.

a Faraday cage suit made of chain mail

On average, 330 people are struck by lightning every year in the United States.

Faraday Cage

British scientist Michael Faraday discovered that a metal cage can protect objects inside from strong electric **currents**. Metal is a good conductor of electricity, so a metal cage carries electric current around the object and discharges it safely to the ground. A car acts like a Faraday cage to keep people inside it safe from lightning.

Park ranger Roy Sullivan survived being struck by lightning seven times in Virginia.

Glossary

2D Stands for two dimensional and means a shape that only has two dimensions (such as width and height) and no thickness.

3D Stands for three dimensional and describes an object that has height, width, and depth, like any object in the real world.

Airbags The safety devices in a car that consist of a bag that inflates automatically in an accident. They prevent the passengers and the driver from being thrown forward.

Antibodies The substances in the blood that can fight off illnesses.

Atoms The smallest particles of a substance that can exist by themselves.

Bacteria Microscopic living things, some of which can cause disease.

Camouflage Coloring or shape that allows something to blend in with its surroundings.

Cells Building blocks or basic units of all living things.

Charge When something is electrically charged it has electricity in it.

Conductors Materials, such as metal, through which electricity can move easily.

Contracts Becomes shorter.

Currents Flows of electricity (or flows of electrons) from one place to another.

Dormant In a state like sleep, not active or growing.

Electrodes The devices that make electrical connections.

Electromagnet A magnet that works only when electric current passes through it.

Electrons Very small parts of an atom, with a negative electric charge.

Evaporates Changes from a liquid to a gas.

Facial expressions Movements or positions of the muscles beneath the skin of the face.

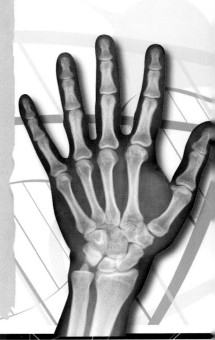

Force A push or a pull.

Force field An invisible barrier of force.

Genes The parts of a cell that influence the appearance or growth of a living thing.

Glands The body parts that release chemical substances.

Immune system The body's system that provides protection from disease and foreign matter.

Insulation Materials that can stop heat, electricity, or sound from escaping.

Interpersonal Between people.

Joints Places where two bones meet on the body.

Life expectancy How long a living thing, such as a person, is expected to live.

Magnetic field The invisible area around a magnet in which the force of magnetism acts.

Magnets Objects or materials that create pushing or pulling forces that can attract or repel (push away) some other objects or materials and other magnets.

Muscle A body part that pulls on bones to make people and other animals move.

Panting Breathing with short noisy gasps.

Paralyzed Unable to move.

Poles Points, such as the ends of a magnet, that have opposing magnetic qualities.

Predators Animals that hunt and eat other animals.

Preservative A substance that stops food or other things from going bad.

Radar A device that sends out radio waves to locate a moving object.

Sensors Devices that sense things such as movement or light.

Stamina Having strength and energy that last a long time.

Static electricity A type of energy that is made when something has too many electrons or protons.

Tai Chi A Chinese system of exercises.

Virus A microscopic living thing that can cause disease.

Yoga Exercises and postures that are designed to promote well-being.

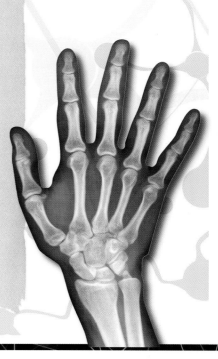

Index